T0193872

Mestizo

Mestizo

A Memoir

L OUIE R ODRIGUEZ

MESTIZO
A MEMOIR

iUniverse books may be ordered through booksellers or by contacting:

iUniverse
1663 Liberty Drive
Bloomington, IN 47403
www.iuniverse.com
1-800-Authors (1-800-288-4677)

ISBN: 978-1-5320-6910-9 (sc)
ISBN: 978-1-5320-6911-6 (e)

Library of Congress Control Number: 2019902840

Print information available on the last page.

iUniverse rev. date: 04/19/2019

Growing Up in Southwest Texas

I remember how beautiful the days of 1944 were. Those days were peaceful, and everyone seemed happy. Even the desert in southwest Texas was beautiful. The skies were vast and clear. The evening sky would look purple at times. There weren't very many trees around, but the ones that existed were very large and commanded attention, especially during the summer, when they were full of leaves. Even though they all looked the same, they were organized in fashion and seemed to stand tall, patrolling the neighborhoods.

The homes were poor. Walls were made from rock, cement, and wood. Even though most homes had electricity and sanitation services, many did not. Most homes didn't have enough furniture to fill them, and there was scarce food and clothing for all. Farther out, you could see mountains and hills. If you were to stand on top of one, you could see the poor border town of Mexico: barren, smoggy, and brown. Houses so poor they were made from cardboard stands.

In the winter, you could smell the fires coming across the border—fires from wood, paper, and even toxic automobile tires being made by the poor peasants in an effort to keep warm. The people of Texas called my run-down neighborhood Segundo Barrio (Second Ward), or, more commonly, Little Mexico. I would think even though we didn't have a lot, we were blessed to have a home, food, and a neighborhood store run by my mother. It was cramped and rickety inside the neighborhood store. An enormous brown fan stood attached to a white wall. A few aisles of yellow shelves proudly supported canned veggies and potted meats. Toward the back of the store, I remember a large icebox with all kinds of meats, steaks, weenies, and chorizos of various sizes. My mother, a frail lady of one hundred pounds, stood behind the counter as strong and independent as ever.

Although my mother was poorly educated, she had an amazing amount of wisdom and kindness. For instance, she would often give store credit to poor families who could not afford food, and she dispensed advice when needed. Many poor families would not have enough money to pay her back. However, being the amazing woman she was, she would never complain and forgave the debts. I now wonder how we got through at times. I always thought that what she lacked in weight, she made up for in brains and kindness. Her large smile and piercing dark eyes will always be etched in my heart.

My father was a go-getter by trade. He worked on anything he could. During his younger days, he worked under the burning sun laying out tracks on a railroad. To me, he seemed to look a lot like Popeye because he was thin but had large, bulky, muscular arms. He was extremely quiet and reserved compared to my mother.

While my mother ran our little store, my father worked setting tile for the houses of white people. He was good at his trade, which was why he was always employed.

My parents came from a small town in Mexico. Like the thousands of poor people who migrated to the United States from Mexico looking for better lives, they also came from very poor families. The Mexican government was so cruel to its people. They never fed the poor, starving, and uneducated Mexicans. They thrived on neglecting the families of emaciated children.

No type of government assistance exists in Mexico. Small children died from malnutrition, and mothers did too. To this day, many Mexican government officials thrive on corruption. Mexico is a third world country, and my parents desperately tried to escape the harsh cruelties associated with it. I was blessed to be born in the United States, and I remember the horror stories told by my elders.

When young, I was content with my life. I lived a life of no luxuries but extreme happiness. Ironically, taking baths was the only thing I hated. Once a week, my mother would fill a giant tin bucket with hot water. She would then tell me, "It's time for your bath, *muchachito* (little boy)." I would instantly resist and tell her no but ultimately would succumb. My mother would wash me with her tiny hands and a large bar of soap. She would then pour warm water over my head. After the bath, she would empty the dirty water and proceed to fill the tin with clean rinsing water. I would come out smelling as fresh as a forest. When we took a bath back in those days, we would use Palmolive bar soap, and it would leave an extremely strong odor on us. I felt so bad for my mother and the other mothers of those times because they had to do a lot of that extra work without the proper facilities.

While growing up in one of the poorest neighborhoods of the city, I had originally thought the whole world was poor like me. I thought that Mexicans were the only race that existed. When I first met an African American, I was scared because I had been used to being around only Mexicans. I didn't know that there were actually people darker than I was.

At home, my mother was a tremendously good cook. She made flour and corn tortillas from scratch, and I remember how tasty they were. They would melt in my mouth, nice and hot, fresh off the griddle and dripping with butter. Back in the day, that was what most Mexican women did.

My younger brother, my sister, and I also grew up on beans, rice, potatoes, and *fideo* soup (a type of long, thin pasta cooked with onions, garlic, and tomato paste). Once a week, we would eat meat and chili. My mother would mix this meat with chili verde, bell peppers, potatoes, onions, garlic, and tomatoes. We would eat this with her delicious homemade tortillas.

At night, my mother would put my siblings and me together to sleep on one bed. Our little apartment consisted of one large room with a kitchen, bathroom, and tiny living room. To us, our mother was as special as a god. We were the little chicks, and my mother was the hen. My father came second. But in Mexican families, the mother is always number one. Maybe it was because they were the nurturers. The father is the provider. Poor Mexican people are very humble, and I believe that comes from our native ancestors, the Indians.

We always had to pray, and I remember having the pleasure of doing so in a big apricot-colored room. The room itself reminded me of the bright homes in Mexico. I would often reminisce about my Mexican upbringing in that little bright room. We were taught to respect elderly people. We'd greet aunts and uncles by kissing their hands or cheeks.

In Mexico

American culture suggested we kiss only on the cheek. However, in Mexico our culture suggested that if you happened to be walking on the same path of a rich man, you'd better pay attention to him. Sometimes you would have to kiss his hand as well, especially the hands of those rich ranch owners.

Most ranch owners treated their employees extremely cruel. In fact, things still seem to be very much the same today. The rich in Mexico have no compassion for the uneducated, poor people. They work the poor with long hours and grant them very little pay. You know the phrase "living paycheck to paycheck." These people didn't even make it to the next paycheck.

Back in my day, the poor ranch employees suffered many harsh beatings as well. A system to protect them from abuse was not enforced. In fact, if these people failed to do their jobs accordingly, the law would not protect them from a proper whack on the head. These people were mistreated just as the African Americans were back in the States. Complaining would cause them to lose their jobs.

Most of them had no choice but to suffer these cruelties in order to feed their wives and children. They were very well controlled down in Mexico. Blood, sweat, and plenty of tears were what plagued their air. These poor people would probably never go to hell when they died because they had suffered enough in their lifetime. That was why these people would cry whenever I witnessed them being deported back to Mexico. Unfortunately, many of them would go like they came into this world, crying. Mexico was God's forgotten country.

In the States, I remember being a kid surrounded by grown people talking about the war era. Aside from the Mexico horror stories, my folks talked about the Japanese War a lot. They were always saying how happy they were that the war was over. My folks said the United States won and would consequently hang a high-ranking Japanese officer, who was flown back to the United States as a POW.

Many people of Japanese descent were placed in concentration camps here in the United States as a result of the war. I could not believe this was being done. Now, in disbelief, it is happening again, only with the Hispanics illegally coming across the border. Children, women, and young boys are being held the same way today, in concentration camps and cages.

Two of my uncles fought in World War II. One came back with the Medal of Honor. We were proud of him for this achievement because we thought this would let people view Mexicans in a more positive manner. Sadly, we had found out it was a mistake to think that way. We were still looked at as greedy Mexicans.

It was amazing that we weren't getting the respect we Mexican Americans should have had for sacrificing and dying for the country we thought we belonged in. Still, we continued our lives as usual with our traditions: family, humility, chili *rellenos*, rice, beans, and tortillas.

Moving on up

In 1953, my sister was eight, my brother was eleven, and I was thirteen. My mother had saved enough money to move us out of the Segundo Barrio neighborhood. Saving all she could from her store earnings, my mother was the brains who controlled all our money. My father knew she had great wisdom with financial matters. He would give her all his paychecks for her to balance. Of course, in those days it wasn't unusual to give your check to your wife to handle. But the man was supposed to handle all other decisions. I am glad that my father thought differently and was okay with my mother handling most of the decisions. Our new piece of land was located in a desolate area. It was out in the boondocks and deserted.

There were hardly any homes on the dry piece of land. Because my father and uncle had experience building homes, they constructed our new home with a few fellow mestizos. My uncles excelled in carpentry, and my father knew how to set brick and tile. My parents finally did it! Our new house consisted of two beautiful bedrooms, two bathrooms, a living room, a kitchen, and a large basement. It had white walls and a spacious backyard for us to play in. The front yard was full of red roses and flowers of various colors that my mother planted. My mother always admired a front yard full of flowers. This was such a peaceful place. In our previous neighborhood of Segundo Barrio, people constantly blasted Mexican music out of their radios, and the noise was extremely annoying. Here, because this land was so deserted, no music was heard anywhere. It was very peaceful and quiet.

During this time, my folks also bought our first refrigerator. The refrigerator seemed very modern because we had previously had only an icebox, which required the constant refilling of ice. What a change. I guess we were going through some modern times. Uncle Carlos, who had previously fought in World War II, would always come to our new home on weekends to visit and sleep over. I distinctly remember my family admiring him for coming home with a Medal of Honor. My brother and I loved him very much. He was so kind and seemed to have a heart bigger than the state of Texas.

Uncle Carlos

My uncle, a man of medium height with a stocky frame, had narrowly escaped death in the horrific war.

While stationed in Japan, he'd fought in hand-to-hand combat—something that is not seen too much anymore, most likely because of the new technology in weapons. Uncle Carlos often fought Japanese soldiers who were highly trained and brutal in inflicting death. Threats of being killed by Japanese swords and combat skills plagued the minds of American soldiers. Aside from that, the Japanese were ready to die if need be, defending their country against the United States. They looked at death as honorable, and they were very loyal to their country.

Being loyal to *his* country, my uncle wasn't about to let the Japanese soldiers intimidate him. He fought hard, as did many other US soldiers, against these skilled warriors. It was said that he succeeded in killing a high-ranking Japanese soldier, choking him to death with his bare hands. He then took his enemy's weapons, a saber sword and a rifle. He had his sword collection displayed inside my mother's house. It was this event that earned him his Medal of Honor. Right next to his sword, Uncle Carlos proudly displayed his medals, which my mom absolutely treasured. While narrowly escaping death, he had been unable to escape the horrible memories of his terrifying and violent ordeals of the war. Today we would call this PTSD.

Uncle Carlos would always bring us candy, comic books, toys, and other items. He dressed like a GI and had a flattop, a military-style haircut. He loved to puff on cigars, and he wore white T-shirts with straight khaki pants and shiny army boots. He was proud to be in the military. He was always smiling and joking, and he had a broad freckled face. Though sometimes he had a look of sadness in his expression, he'd never let that take hold of him.

Whenever he'd enter the house with his cigar lit, he knew he had to extinguish it before my mother saw him because she would chew him up alive. My mother hated the smell of cigars. After a while of joking around, my uncle would say, "Okay, guys, you and your brother get out the boxing gloves." He had brought us shiny new leather boxing gloves.

Every week, he would teach my brother and me how to box. He would kneel a little so that our punches could reach him better. Then he would act like he was trying to hit us, and he would intentionally miss so that we could learn how to dodge and weave. Sometimes he would put his face in front of me on purpose so that I could hit him.

As a kid, I hit him a few times, and he would retaliate with, "Hit me harder!" I didn't want to hurt my uncle even though I knew he was purposely letting himself get hit like a punching bag. Some days I noticed he had tears in his eyes, as if remembering something in his past. As I think about it now, I presume he was having flashbacks of his experiences in the war. My uncle taught us boxing so that we would be able to protect ourselves from the bullies we might encounter at school.

When we would finish with our boxing lessons, my mother would say, "Come and eat pronto, before the food gets cold." She would then ask where my father was, and we would run to find him. After boxing, we usually ate chicken tacos with lots of lettuce, cheese, and chunks of some homegrown tomatoes. I guess my mother assumed we needed extra protein after a boxing match.

Uncle Carlos was a champion eater. Wow, he could sure eat! My mother would comment that he often could eat one or two whole chickens. We couldn't help but laugh as my uncle chowed down a dozen tacos. "Hey, leave some tacos for us, *hermano*!" my mother would kid. Good thing we always had plenty of chickens in the backyard.

Regarding the chicken tacos, my mother would always use fresh chickens. Back in the day, it wasn't unusual to raise chickens in one's backyard. She would tell Uncle Carlos to go into our backyard and get two or three chickens for the whole family to eat. My uncle would proceed to get one chicken at a time. Afterward, he'd roughly karate chop it to the neck. Once the chicken was dead, he would place it inside the sink.

My mother would then gently pluck its feathers. The little feathers my mom was unable to pluck would be burned using a rolled-up newspaper and some fire. After a good washing, the chicken was ready to be cooked and stuffed into our delicious tacos. I'll always cherish those beautiful memories I had with my uncle and my beautiful family.

Painful Times

Painful moments often accompanied those beautiful moments in life, however. Our happy days were vastly turning into a nightmare as my uncle's hourglass quickly began to run low of sand. In fact, although he had escaped death while fighting the dangerous Japanese soldiers, fate would have Uncle Carlos die at the hands of the savage Mexican police.

Since his return from the war, Uncle Carlos had suffered from recurring nightmares. He could not sleep, and as a result, he resorted to drinking heavily. One night he entered a bar. The bar was about to close, and he still hadn't had his fix of alcohol. He quickly walked across the border to Mexico, to the place where bars were always open.

Slightly buzzed, he walked into a bar, sat in the corner, and ordered another drink by himself. He was minding his own business, as usual. The night went by, and after several hours, a fight broke out next to him. Because this was such a disturbance, the police were summoned. They barged into the bar with full fury and a mentality of not caring who started the fight. They began to violently swing their nightsticks and blackjacks (which at the time were very popular for cops to use) at everybody inside the bar. Even innocent bystanders were getting their heads bashed in. These lead-filled sticks were very deadly, and many people fell to the floor, seriously injured. In fact, blackjacks were notorious for breaking skulls.

They say my uncle was in the corner and consuming a drink when the cops spotted him and started to rough him up. The crowd surrounding them began to protest in anger that my uncle had nothing to do with the fight. The cops paid no attention. My uncle, being a warrior from war, was not able to stand this type of treatment. He began to fight back to protect himself.

The cops, savage in nature, probably caused him to have a flashback of the war. The vicious fight continued but to no avail. The cops violently bashed my uncle with their heavy blackjacks. They say there were five cops against my unarmed uncle, who stood alone. They attacked my uncle like a pack of wild wolves trying to kill their prey. His blood spattered everywhere, and by the end of the attack, there was nothing but a mangled corpse on the floor with his head split open by police brutality.

My wonderful uncle, the amazing war hero. Here he lay dead in a sleazy Mexican bar. His body was motionless on a dirty floor, and the blood seeping from his lacerated head contributed to the filth of the atmosphere. It seems all very repulsive and surreal to think about. Yet it seems ironic that what the Japanese were unable to do, the Mexican cops were able to do: kill him.

After his death, the police dragged Uncle Carlos's body to the police station and stole his money and gold wristwatch. They then transported his body to some sand dunes far away from the city and began to search his pockets to see what else they could leach off him. It was then where they realized that they had killed a US citizen. Still, they didn't seem to care.

A writer, wanting to remain anonymous, had found out this information and related it to my family. He feared the Mexican police killing him or his family, so he tried to remain as secretive as possible. Of course, he related that the only police report found of the incident was fabricated and stated that my uncle's body was missing and couldn't be found. Thanks to witnesses who saw the fight, we knew that the police had been the ones who'd murdered my uncle. Still, no one had given us a body.

My parents were completely devastated by the horrible crime. We loved Uncle Carlos so much. At that time, Aunt Luz (Uncle Carlos's sister) contacted a high-ranking officer from the US military. We desperately wanted his body back. Within a few days, the US military contacted Aunt Luz and told her that they had contacted the Mexican authorities, who had then "miraculously" found my uncle's body. We were told his body was to be transferred back to the States for a decent military burial. After further negotiation with the Mexican authorities, Uncle Carlos's body was cleared to come back into the country.

I remember the day was very chilly and sad. We were all standing, waiting on the border bridge that connects the United States with Mexico. After several minutes, we caught a glimpse of a big black hearse coming from the other side of the bridge. The whole situation seemed like a horrible nightmare.

His funeral would be closed casket because his body was badly disfigured. The military also informed us that there would be a memorial for my uncle for all who wanted to say their final goodbyes. A day later, my uncle was buried with full military honors. My family and I felt terrible and had already begun to miss him. We remembered his smiling freckled face and his kind heart. God had taken him to the beautiful garden up above. Time would never heal the wounds we suffered from losing Uncle Carlos.

High School

My brother, my sister, and I were growing up fast. We were already teenagers, and still we wanted to be older. Go figure. We thought that as teenagers, we knew everything there was to know about life. The isolated location of our house was no longer isolated. In the mid-1950s, more new homes sprung up everywhere around our home. Funny enough, Anglo-Americans were moving into our new neighborhood in droves. This made us the minority. My siblings and I had to go to the nearest schools, which also happened to have a mostly Anglo population. My sister was sent to a grade school while my brother and I enrolled in high school.

We were surprised to experience little discrimination. In fact, all the teachers were kind and helpful. They came across as good human beings. Of course, we did come across the occasional white kid who did not like Latinos. I found myself always having to defend myself.

Right before my fifteenth birthday, I had enrolled in some boxing lessons from an ex–professional boxer named Luis. This Cuban boxer had fought out of Mexico. While boxing one day, he had been hurt to the point of blindness. After retiring, he continued with his training. Although blind, he would train me and show me the style of how he would throw his punches. For a man in his fifties, his body was well toned. He was a fighter, and although blind, he could still hit the light and heavy bags If they were lined up next to him. Hearing the force of his fists against the bag, I knew he had a good, hard punch. I was very delighted with his willingness to teach me more about boxing. He taught me things Uncle Carlos didn't get a chance to teach me. I will always remember him. I became obsessed with all kinds of self-defense tactics. I even began to study judo from a book.

To my surprise, despite not having a personal instructor, I did quite well. I would go over the illustrated pictures of different holds in my mind at night. By golly, they did work when it came time. Later on, I met a martial artist, and he explained that it was possible to learn from a good book. For a lot of moves, all you have to do is pinpoint them in your mind over and over, and the mind guides the body.

I took a lot of his self-defense courses. In no time, I grew from a frail little kid into a strong one who was capable of defending himself. I would often get bullied in grade school, and by the time high school arrived, I was tired of it. It was much like a commercial I remember, where a character repeatedly gets beach sand kicked in his face. After every lesson, I left more confident.

One of the biggest bullies in my high school was named Johnny, and the other was Richie. Johnny was trouble. When he was walking in the hallways of the school, you'd better get out of his way. Johnny was mean and would bump you out of the way if he came across you. All the other kids were frightened of him. He was a good-sized kid for fifteen, and he had a head of thick red hair. He looked vicious with his mean blue eyes of steel. I always tried my best to get out of his way like the others because I didn't want any trouble.

Of course, avoiding him finally caught up with me one day. A lot of us guys were heading for the locker room before P.E. one day. We were going to suit up and put on our gym clothes. The gym room was overcrowded, and Coach Manny, a short but well-built man, entered the room and began barking orders like a military sergeant. When he finished, he concluded with, "I will be right back, you guys. Sit down on those benches and wait for me."

Coach Manny left the locker room. There were too many of us, and we couldn't all sit down on the small number of benches. I had to stand with a few other guys while Johnny the bully got to sit down on a bench. After a while, he decided to leave the bench with a few other guys to go horse-around. Because he'd left the bench, I decided to sit on it.

It wasn't but a few minutes when he returned and was angry. Johnny yelled, "Get out of my seat, wetback!"

I instantly got a little nervous. After all, this was Johnny the Beast we were talking about. I said to myself, *What the hell did I get myself into?* I started to get up from the bench when Johnny decided to slug me on the side of my face. I don't know what happened to my mind, but I instantly started throwing left and right hooks without even thinking. I knocked him off balance and caught him by surprise. Nobody had ever dared raise a hand to him. He tried to come at me again, but I had confidence that I had been well trained by both Uncle Carlos and my Cuban friend Luis.

I threw a perfect right hand to his forehead. Instantly his eyes rolled back in his head, and I knew I had him. It was at that point when Coach

Manny walked back into the P.E. room. "What the hell is going on here?" he yelled. "You guys want to fight? I'll fix that right now!" He went and got some old, stale-looking boxing gloves so that we could beat the crap out of each other.

"Are you ready, Louie?" he asked with a face full of anger.

"Coach … it's just that Johnny and I really don't want to fight," I said reluctantly.

"Well, what the hell! It looked like you guys were throwing punches. Weren't *you*, Johnny?" asked Coach Manny.

"Aw, we were just playing, Coach," said Johnny, trying to sound friendly.

Coach Manny scoffed. "That's why you got that unicorn horn on your forehead," he said. All the other guys started laughing. "Well, we're not having any more fights here. And you, Johnny—I've noticed you have been bullying a few guys. You got what you deserve. Next time, I'll have Louie beat the crap out of you again." Coach had a sly grin on his face. I never thought Coach Manny would back me up.

After P.E. was finished, the class and I headed out to our separate class schedules. The other guys started to surround me in the hallway exclaiming, "Hey, where did you learn to fight like that? Teach us!" Now they all wanted to be my friends. Of course, I owed it all to Uncle Carlos and my friend Luis. These kids were really impressed.

The next day, at school, I met Richie. Richie was fifteen and much bigger than Johnny. Richie had heard what I had done to Johnny and began to harass me for it. "I heard you are pretty tough, punk!" he said through gritted teeth. "Do you want to try to fight me?"

I responded with a "Heck, no!" and started to run away. This guy looked scary.

He was a little short of six feet tall. As I ran, Richie chased me all through the crowded hallways. I was a fast runner, and Richie was getting frustrated that he couldn't catch me. I finally made it into a classroom with Richie right behind me, huffing and puffing. He was steaming mad by now.

Mrs. Smith, the teacher standing at the door of the classroom, asked Richie if this was the classroom he was supposed to be at. "No," he answered. Mrs. Smith said, "Then get your butt where you are supposed to be." I started to chuckle to myself because it sure was funny. Richie's face was as red as a beet. For the next two weeks, Richie kept trying to hunt me down, but I was too clever and fast for the guy.

One day, I goofed up and saw Richie in the hallway again. My eyes scanned for an escape route, but to my horror, I saw nothing but a boy's restroom in front of me. I quickly entered the restroom, a large room consisting of five urinals and three stalls. I could imagine that Richie had figured he had finally trapped me. I backed away from the entrance as Richie ran in like a raging bull.

"Okay, punk! I've finally got you!" he said as he rushed toward me and grabbed me by the collar. He slammed my body hard against the wall behind me and began to punch me. Out of fear, I punched back like crazy. My punches were automatic—I was swinging my left and right fists at a dashing speed. I could see his punches, but I felt mine coming out faster than his. I owed this all to my boxing practices. After a while, I caught Richie with a punch to his ribs. He grunted and went down to his knees. He grabbed his stomach in pain and collapsed onto the floor, crying. I was in awe at what I saw. Don't get me wrong—I really did feel bad for poor Richie. I reached down and helped him up. I even hugged him and told him I was sorry for kicking his butt like that.

To my surprise, he opened up and told me that the reason he was crying was because of the humiliation he had suffered of having a smaller guy defeat him. Richie felt bad, but I tried to comfort him the best I could. I told him that he did a good job and was actually pretty tough. After that,

Richie and I became good friends, and worked together as a team. We would back each other up if any of us ever got into any fights.

After a while, other teenagers took notice and decided not to mess with us. We knew we were good at fighting, and in our overconfidence, we overlooked the fact that we had become bullies. We were at a point where we thought we could beat up any teenager we came across. Of course, we never realized that in life, you'll always run into someone tougher than you are.

After a day of pushing some kids around, I bumped into this tiny Mexican boy. We had an exchange of words and got angry with one another. We began to fight and, in an instant this little kid had me down. He was tougher than I'd thought. I'd finally met my match, and he beat the crap out of me. Right there and then, I learned not to be the bully I had become.

Teenage Years

I dropped out of high school after my freshman year. I simply wasn't able to handle the course load. My mom was extremely disappointed, but she didn't let me sleep around like a bum. I remember the day after I told her, she woke me up the next morning at five by blasting her record player outside of my bedroom door. "*Mijo*," she said, "it's time to start looking for a job."

I was angry and kind of in shock by the whole act. I guess looking for a job to support myself had never entered my mind. After a day of looking, I came across a grocery store. As a kid, I was terrified to go in and ask for a job. I timidly entered, spotted the manager, and asked him if they had any open positions. He told me that I could start as soon as tomorrow, and just like that, I had my very first job as a grocery store bagger. It was so easy to get a job back then.

By 1956, I was sixteen years old. I remember going to drive-in movies with my guys, and we would all chip in for beer. We had a guy who looked twenty-one years old. He was the one in charge of getting the beer for us, and after drinking at the drive-in, we would all go over the border bridge to Mexico to continue partying. In Mexico, at the time, they didn't care if we drank underage as long as we had the money to pay for it. The guys knew I had a job, so whenever my payday came, they would hit me up. We never took into consideration the dangers that lurked in the dark. Everything seemed innocent to us. We were so naïve. It seems like youth never sense danger.

Down in Mexico, various neon bar signs attracted our attention. One in particular had a "Carta Blanca" beer on it. The nightlife wanted to reach out and grab us. Beautiful girls kept calling out to us, "Come on, muchachos! I will show you a good time!" In every door, a beautiful girl tried to lure us inside. After a while, we entered a bar with American music playing in the background. The walls inside were a dark red color, and it looked a little creepy. Still, we hung around and had a couple of drinks.

Everybody in there looked so old to us. They were all very quiet and mysterious adults. We began to feel uneasy and unsafe and decided to get out of there. The second we did so, a fight erupted between the bartender and a client. They really got into it, and to make matters worse, they both had knives. It was terrible, and we had never seen anything like that; we were too young. They knifed each other very brutally, and blood spattered all over the place. Both were yelling and hollering. It reminded me of a Roman gladiator showdown. All of a sudden, the guy the bartender was stabbing had enough and staggered out the door. Everybody inside was cheering and hugging the bloody bartender. People even went as far as to exclaim he was a hero. I couldn't believe this. I told my friends that we had to get the hell out of there before anything else happened.

One year later, we had another friend who convinced us to go to Mexico again. He told us to forget about last year's incident and assured us it wouldn't happen again. He said he knew about an extremely peaceful place where we could go and drink beer. Being ignorant, we believed him and headed off to the red-light district in Mexico. As we started to approach the clubs, we encountered the all-too-familiar sight of the beautiful girls calling out to us. We approached a nightclub named Delicious. Inside, we bought drinks for all the girls, and there were loads of laughter and fun. We stayed in there for hours, drinking and talking with the various types of Mexican girls.

As we were about to leave, an older man walked inside. He looked like he was in his forties, and he seemed intoxicated. He began to cry and plead to one of the girls in there to come home with him. He fell to his knees and began to make a big scene. The girl told him to leave, but he continued to plead. Instantly three gangster-looking guys dressed up in hats and brightly colored suits approached this man and hit him with their blackjacks. They wacked him all over his body and head so routinely that it seemed as if this was a normal activity for them. Still, regardless of how many blows he received, the poor guy would not subside. He wasn't even hollering.

Inside, I was screaming. Why wouldn't they stop beating him? These people were so cruel. I couldn't believe that this was happening right in front of me. After a while, I figured the guy was probably dead. Yet the men continued to beat his corpse to make sure he really was dead, or so I figured. My mind at the time could not conceive of such a thing happening. It all seemed like a bad dream. These cruel, cold-blooded monsters had to have no conscience to destroy a human life like that. I hoped that these men were someday sent to hell for committing such a heartless act.

I also remember wishing that God would not forgive these evil men for what they did. The image of the man's lifeless and dismantled body stood in my mind for a long time. I even cried for the man some nights. It took years for me to move on from the horrific memories of the incident. I wondered about Uncle Carlos and what all he must have witnessed when he was at war. I told myself I would never visit Mexico again; the memories there were just too bad, and the country seemed to be violent and dangerous. I saw no interest in sacrificing my safety for it. It was a country where shootouts occurred daily in the middle of the streets between cops and drug dealers. Innocent bystanders in the way were often shot, and they were left in the streets to rot until the heartless police with no conscience decide to pick up the bodies. The Mexican police could care less about public safety.

Alicia's Wedding

I remember there was a day when my mother told my brother and me about my cousin Alicia's wedding. The wedding was to take place in Southern California. We didn't have the money to go, but my cousin Alicia was kind enough to send us bus tickets to go to her wedding. My brother and I were anxious to go, and I told him that before we got too excited, we would have to ask our boss for permission to leave for a few days. "You know how our supervisor gets if you want a day off," I remember telling my brother.

Mr. Hacin always asked rudely why anyone would want a day off. "It's better to work seven days a week—you get richer!" was his familiar response. To our surprise, he actually approved us for one week off. We weren't expecting that. The next day, my brother and I went straight to the local station. My parents had changed their minds about going; they were getting too old and felt tired lately. I completely understood. All of this added a bigger sense of adventure to our trip. These were bus trips that Mexicans straight out of Mexico would take to work in the fields of California. I mentioned this fact to my brother, and we both chuckled a bit.

The Greyhound bus we were on was extremely comfortable. The seats were soft, fluffy, and roomy. Back then, everything was made so much better. The Greyhound seats of today are made of tough, flat material that leaves one's butt sore; it's like riding on a horse's back. We rode smoothly for several hours and drove passed the ugly desert, which was so dry and lonely.

After what seemed like an eternity, the bus made a stop at a building with a ton of lights on it. Through the bus windows, we could see a tall, slender Anglo man dressed in his border patrol outfit standing right outside of the bus. The Greyhound driver quickly opened the door to let him in, and he carefully examined everybody sitting down. Now, it was just our luck to be on a bus filled with Anglos as opposed to one filled with Mexicans. Because of this, my brother and I stuck out like sore thumbs, and the man's eyes quickly landed on us. His blue eyes stared at us intensely. Hateful and coldly, he approached us. In Spanish he asked us where our papers were.

Everybody in the bus turned around to stare at us joyfully. It was as if they were mentally saying, "All right! Finally these wetbacks are going to get busted!"

"Andale! Pronto!" the border patrol agent shouted angrily.

"Yes, sir!" I responded.

"You speak good English. Where did you learn it?" he asked.

"Well, I was brought up in this country. Here's my ID," I said. After looking at my ID, he asked for my brother's. My brother showed his ID to him. He nodded, handed my brother back his ID, and turned and left the bus.

The feeling in the bus shifted to an uncomfortable one; I sensed the other Anglos were not too happy he'd left us on the bus. They'd expected the border patrol agent to escort us off but got nothing in return. I thought, *What if there were illegal Asians, Russians, or Germans on the bus?*

Because the other people on the bus were white, this agent didn't even bother to check their IDs. They forgot that there were many Hispanics that were fair skinned too. The right and proper thing to do would have been to ask everybody to show their identification cards. A good border patrol agent would have done that. Times were so different then. Hatred for Latinos was great. It seems like this hatred is escalating once again. Is history repeating itself? Sometimes I wonder. In that time, there seemed to be no respect for many Hispanics, even though many had died fighting for this country in World War II.

After several more hours had passed and night had shifted into day, we arrived in Southern California. I looked out the window of the bus and was greeted with nothing but beautiful green trees and shrubbery covering the landscape. Wow, what a change! It was stunning. Before we knew it, we were pulling into the local station.

The bus driver began yelling, "We are in the city of Los Angeles. Thank you all very much for riding with us!" All the passengers began to jump out of their seats and grab their suitcases. Everybody wanted to be the first one out, like always. My brother and I took our time getting out of the bus. After making our way off the bus, our bodies aching and our butts tired, we began to breathe the fresh California air. Loads of people around us were meeting with their relatives and hugging them tightly.

We were having a hard time getting past the crowd of cheerful people. We trudged forward, looking everywhere to see if we could spot my cousin. While bumping into numerous elbows and shoulders, we moved slowly. Finally, we made our way inside the less-crowded station and found a seat to sit on. My brother and I chatted for a while. After about twenty minutes, I looked up and saw this wavy- and dirty-blonde-haired woman looking at us, trying to recognize who we were. We looked at her in turn, trying to process whether this was our dear cousin Alicia, whom I hadn't seen since my childhood. I got up and walked toward the woman. She began to smile as she asked, "You're Louie, right?"

"Yes," I said, smiling back. "And over there is Romulo."

I hugged her. Alicia had grown into a beautiful woman. She was in her early twenties and had a bright complexion with a slender build. Her clothes matched her grace, and her long, wavy hair seemed to dance with charm. I couldn't believe nature. I could still see the little girl in her face. My brother came over and hugged her as well. We had so much to talk about because we hadn't seen her in years. She led us outside of the bus station to her gleaming blue Chrysler.

"Cousin!" I exclaimed. "You're doing very well! I congratulate you."

"Thank you," she responded, smiling. "And I also thank God, who has helped me much." She had gotten a good education and eventually became a lawyer. That was amazing for a Mexican American woman to do at the time. It turned out she was helped a lot by a California program that helped minorities seeking a higher education. They helped minorities out more in California than in Texas. In Texas, it seemed that the discrimination against Mexicans was too great. At times, I felt the state didn't want us to succeed at all.

Man, that Chrysler could move! We roared through the freeway like a jet. Californians drove very fast, and that Chrysler had no problem keeping up. The windows were down, and the summer air blew through our hair. We smelled the Pacific Ocean in the air, and it was all very wonderful.

When the car stopped, we were greeted with a beautiful home designed with a Mexican style. Outside were many pots of different colored flowers. We took a second to take in everything and then headed inside with all our things. For hours we chatted in the living room about the family and the things going on around us. When it got late, my cousin said we'd better get some sleep. The wedding would take place the next day, and the church was going to conduct mass in the morning. My cousin showed us to our rooms, and before we knew it, we were fast asleep.

The next morning, we got ready and headed for church. Once there, we met with some family I had never seen before. Some came from Mexico, and others came from other parts of California. Everyone was dressed very well. Women and young girls looked very pretty with all their new dresses. Men walked confidently, sporting handsome suits. My brother and I blended in with the crowd because we had also brought with us nice clothing. We met the groom, a tall and slender guy with a short, clean-cut haircut. We were very happy to meet him. He was a Mexican guy in his early twenties. He smiled and told us his name was Thomas. Looking to his left, we could see Alicia dressed in a beautiful white wedding dress. Various colored roses were spread throughout the church.

As I looked at them, I hoped that my cousin had chosen the right guy. Thomas was from a well-off family in Mexico; I believe he was an engineer. My cousin seemed very happy, and we wished her well. I thought to myself, *I hope one day I will meet a good woman in my life.* We took our seats and looked at the old priest walking to the altar. The wedding was beginning, and everybody took their positions.

After a couple of minutes, my cousin, the bride, slowly started walking to the altar. The music played gracefully in the background. The atmosphere inside was filled with a lot of emotion; I could see it on everybody's face. Some people's eyes were filled with tears, like in the movies. Alicia had finally reached the altar, and after exchanging vows, they were joined together by the priest. They kissed, and just like that, they were married. It was quite sentimental.

Upon leaving the church, we were met with a lot of confetti being thrown at us and toward the bride and groom. Everybody was laughing and crying. Alicia and Thomas joyfully emerged from the church holding each other's hands. They were escorted into a big black Cadillac while everybody was cheering and clapping. It was an amazing wedding.

When night fell, my brother and I headed to the reception hall. This hall was a large white building with glass doors and Spanish-style frames. It was located right in the heart of Los Angeles. As we walked inside, we noticed lots of tables with white tablecloths. Many people were sitting and laughing, enjoying the festivities. Small children were playing in the center of the dance floor. The floors themselves were varnished with a beautiful brown color.

When the food had all been consumed, the lights were dimmed and the music was turned up. Alicia and her new husband began to dance, and everybody clapped. It was very enjoyable for everyone. While everybody danced, I noticed there were a lot of pretty girls with shimmering black hair. I winked at my little brother and asked him what he thought. He responded, "These are good-looking broads!" We laughed as we sipped on a couple of piña coladas. The music of the time period was the most angelic one can imagine. I remember hearing "Love Is a Many Splendored Thing" by the Four Aces.

I noticed one female giving me the eye. She had very pretty hazel eyes and shoulder-length dark hair. *What the heck!* I told myself. I got up and walked over to her table. She was surrounded by a bunch of other beautiful girls. I leaned in and asked her if she would like to dance. To my enjoyment, she accepted.

We danced for a while, her body that of a well-formed young lady. Afterward, we talked for a long while and danced again. When we were tired of dancing, we talked some more. We talked about everything, and it all seemed to be going so well until this big ugly thug tapped me on the shoulder. He stated that it was *his* turn to dance with her. "You know this guy?" I asked the girl. She quickly said no and expressed concern that she didn't want to dance with him.

This guy seemed half-intoxicated and on drugs. Additionally, he was dressed like a pachuco. Pachucos were notoriously known for carrying knives with them, so I knew he had to be dangerous. Many were worthless crooks who made our race look bad. I could tell this girl was beginning to feel afraid. "Sorry, guy," I said to the thug. "It doesn't look like she wants to dance with you." I could see the mean expression on his face.

"You punk!" he yelled at me, and before I knew it, I felt a hit on my neck. My knees buckled and I was rapidly knocked onto the ground. I heard the poor girl screaming. I felt dazed and couldn't really get up. This ugly pachuco continued to hit me and kick my ribs. I thought my life was over and could imagine the feeling of his knife slicing through my body. Just as I was about to abandon all hope of survival, I heard a loud bang followed by the enormous thud of the pachuco coming down next to me.

It was my little brother! He had wacked that monster with a chair. Thank God that my brother was there for the rescue. The pachuco was out cold. As I slowly got up, I noticed another ugly pachuco running toward us. I kicked him right in his family jewels, and my brother gave him a karate chop to the back of the neck. He went down just as fast as the other guy. I was very proud of my brother. We were stuck in a very embarrassing situation.

My cousin and her husband came running toward us. "What happened, Cousin?" she asked with a frightened tone. "Are you okay, Louie?" I explained to them what had happened. As I looked over my cousin's shoulder, I saw the cops coming into the building. These guys were both big and hefty. An elder gentleman was explaining to the cops the situation while they walked on over. When they came toward me, they asked me to explain to them what had happened. I told them what had occurred and that nothing was my or my brother's fault. The cops looked at us and then at the crooks on the floor. Then to my satisfaction, they picked up the pachucos like bags of potatoes. The thugs squealed like pigs when the cops twisted their arms to put their handcuffs on. As they dragged them away, I felt blood come out of my nose. Other than that and my neck being a little sore, I was okay, thank God.

The girl I was dancing with came up to tell me how sorry she was that this had happened. I told her that it wasn't her fault and that she shouldn't feel bad. I mean, I sure wasn't going to let her get abused by that punk. After that, we hit it off very well. Her name was Betty, and it turned out she was good friends with my cousin. After the incident, my cousin invited her over to her house. In addition to that, my cousin invited a few more guests. I was excited because I had met my first real girlfriend.

After an hour, all of us were gathered inside Alicia's pretty house. We were all in the living room, which had very attractive furniture and a beautiful coffee-colored table in the middle of the room. We enjoyed each other's company that night and met more family members whom we had not known. Standing out above the others was this old man in a gray suit. He was slim and had a smiling face. "Hola!" he said, extending his hand. "My name is Hugo." Hugo was from Mexico. He looked high class and distinguished.

"My name is Louie," I responded, "and this is my brother, Romulo."

"Mucho Gusto. Nice to meet you!" We began to chat. I remember asking him if he lived in Mexico. He said that he had lived there all his life. In fact, he had a business over there. We had a couple of tequila shots after that.

Now, before taking a shot of tequila, it is Mexican custom to say, "Salud." This is like saying, "Cheers." Hugo began to tell me stories about Mexico.

He asked me if I was Mexican American, and I said yes but added that my parents were from a small town in Mexico. He smiled and told me he had been to the town my parents were from several times. I told him my parents had migrated to the United States some time ago. They'd wanted a better life for their children, like most parents did. Hugo began to get embarrassed as he offered an apology for his government.

"I can't blame your parents. The United States is such a wonderful country. My Mexican government unfortunately has much corruption," he said. "It has many bad flaws; I have to admit this. It is sad that we will never be able to correct this situation. The few who are extremely rich and powerful control the country. The few who want to do something for their people get eliminated from the system. It's so very bad. A lot is happening in Mexico." Hugo looked down. He then told me of Anglos getting kidnapped and held for ransom. He said there was no law that would protect anybody in Mexico, which enabled kidnappers to get richer and richer. He then talked about Pancho Villa and how he always helped the poor. Pancho Villa was a villain to the Mexican government because he stole from the rich and gave to the poor—a kind of Robin Hood.

In a way, I guess it was good in the old days when Pancho Villa existed, even though he murdered corrupt politicians and dignitaries who hurt the poor. Back then, the wealthy hated Pancho Villa, and I know that they still do to this day. The poor Mexicans were emaciated and starving to death while the rich were getting richer with their corrupt ways and corrupt government. Nobody was helping the poor except for Pancho Villa.

In fact, stories tell that Pancho Villa would cut off the ears of wealthy Spaniards. He got his message across with fear, which in turn caused many of Mexico's foreigners to run away from the country. They were terrified of this man and his cronies. I began to talk about how I supported what Pancho Villa did, and many people in the room looked at me funny. Alicia made a slight coughing sound, and I took that as a hint that I had said enough. Like I said, to this day, many still hate Pancho Villa.

Hugo asked me if I had ever heard of a woman in Mexico they had called La Nacha. I said I could slightly remember my folks mentioning her name when I was little. "Yes!" he said. "La Nacha was a mean and powerful woman. The United States was pretty upset at Mexico for not breaking her. They used to call her the Marijuana Queen, which she was. She had connections with some of the American mafia men." Hugo also said that her headquarters was in Mexico. She had an in-depth knowledge on drugs and was very intelligent.

That was just one of the many exciting stories Hugo seemed to be filled with that evening. My brother and I listened to many interesting stories about Mexico that night. My family was very fortunate to be in this country, even though we suffered from discrimination. When you were an underdog like us, you simply had to do the best you could and put everything else in the hands of God.

After the party, I began to reminisce about some of the stories my parents would tell me about their childhood. I remembered my dad mentioning the depression days of the 1930s. He said a lot of rich people who had lost their financial estates were jumping off buildings. He also said that although we were extremely poor, nobody in our family had ever killed themselves. These rich people couldn't survive and were too weak to be poor. What a shame! To be poor is sometimes a great experience in life. The days when you go hungry and sleep cold can build strength, resilience, and character from within. If you survive these hard times, you will fully understand and appreciate life. We came from a poor Mexican family, and I am glad I learned so much as a result. I am glad I did not come from a rich environment. I would have hated to be a spoiled, rich brat.

The next day, Alicia drove my brother and me to the local bus station. We said our goodbyes and wished her the best for her future. After watching her car speed away, we looked at the bus that was approaching the terminal. It was time to go home.

Young Man

By the mid-1960s, all my friends were out of high school, and the Vietnam era rapidly approached us. The time was very vicious because there were many men my age being brought back from the war dead.

Many Mexicans were also being killed in the war. In 1969, Selective Service summoned me to register for the draft. I was only twenty-eight years old, and my mother was terrified. Many guys who were in my position went into hiding. Some fled to Canada and others to Mexico. I couldn't judge them because it was a very scary time to be alive. I remember thinking to myself, *If they call me to war, will I be as brave as my uncle Carlos was in the Second World War?* I could already picture myself being called in for duty. I have to admit the thought terrified the daylights out of me. I was ready to serve my country like my brave uncle had, but that didn't leave me fearless.

When I was finally called into the Selective Service office, many of my friends who had been previously summoned to the war before me had come back home in pine boxes. All around us, mothers and fathers were left to cry over their dead sons. After registering for the draft, I was called back into the office to go through a physical. In the physical, they told me I could not go to war because I was flat-footed. What? I thought that was odd. I felt bad because I had finally begun to think that I could have made it out alive. At the same time, I felt guilty in thinking about my friends who were sent to Vietnam while I was not. In late 1969, my little brother was called to register for the draft too. I began to pray very hard that he would not have to go.

I guess it's weird because there are times where our prayers aren't answered exactly how we would expect. My little brother ended up having to go to Vietnam. A group of some more of my high school friends did too. While they were gone, I dedicated every night to pray for their safety. To my relief, the majority of them came back from Vietnam in one piece. God brought them back home safely, and I was so grateful. Some of them weren't so lucky though. Some came back handicapped, and others came back like my uncle Carlos. I felt really bad for them.

When my brother came back from Vietnam, I was working at a factory run by some Arabs. I was able to get my brother a job there, and in no time, we were able to rent an apartment together. We were getting too old to continue living with our parents, and we desperately wanted a place to call our own. We would still visit my parents every weekend, and if they were lucky, we'd show up with some groceries in hand.

My siblings and I were finally grown adults. My sister had married an Anglo boy. My brother and I worried that she had not chosen the right man. I didn't know where she had met this young man. With all the discrimination going on, I wondered where she had found him. We were all a little broken up at the news, especially my parents. I hoped and prayed very hard that this man would treat my sister right.

His name was Lloyd, and he was from some town in Tennessee. I remember thinking, *Oh brother! I hope he doesn't take her away from here to some place in Tennessee!* That would be the worst place to take a Mexican girl. If racism was bad in Texas, just think of how much worse it would be in Tennessee! My sister had turned out to be a beautiful girl with a pretty olive complexion. She had long, shiny black hair.

She and Lloyd rented an apartment in the same neighborhood we'd lived in as kids. It seemed funny that they would go back to that neighborhood. I began to try to piece the puzzle together. Lloyd was probably an outcast from his race; that was the only answer. My sister would tell me that Lloyd would like a good breakfast consisting of two eggs with enchiladas. She would set the plate for him on a small wooden table that they'd probably bought at the used furniture store. Their apartment was small and poor, and my sister would always serve Lloyd a nice warm plate of food. Her smile was as big as the Texas sky. It made her happy to be appreciated by her husband. How they'd met was a mystery. They were both from two different worlds, and I could never grasp how Lloyd could be in love with a Mexican girl. My sister told me they often fought about paying their rent. I guess she should have married a man with more financial responsibility.

One evening, my sister told me that she was trying to help Lloyd find a job. The rent money was coming up short, and my parents couldn't help her pay it. When she brought up the subject, he would stop smiling and grow angry. "Why don't you go see Mr. Sonny? He's got a moving van business," said my sister. "How about it, Lloyd?"

Lloyd looked bothered. "Okay," he responded hesitantly, "but I'll have to borrow some more money today to catch the bus. What if he says no?"

"Then I'll get you a job downtown. I have a friend who works there and can help," responded my sister, Mena. "The bus isn't that expensive; I think two dollars should be sufficient." Mena stared hard into Lloyd's face. A disappointed look spread upon Lloyd's face, as well as Mena's. "My family thinks you're trying, Lloyd … but not hard enough," said Mena. "Please don't embarrass me again." I guess we had a cultural belief that Anglo men were supposed to be hardworking and successful. Mena asked Lloyd, "What happened to you? You've disappointed me. You promised me you would try. Look what you've given me. It's by far a shame!"

Tears fell from Mena's beautiful eyes. "You are a disgrace to your people. I know well that your parents never wanted you to marry a Mexican girl. You told me yourself. We Mexicans took you in and never once discriminated against you. My family and people in the barrio always treated you with respect."

"Okay, I will go see Mr. Sonny!" shouted Lloyd angrily. "This hard labor is fit for Mexicans, but not for me! How the hell did I get into this damned mess?"

In the 1970s, Texas began to change. I started seeing Mexican American boys and girls finishing high school. In fact, it became a norm to finish high school. These high school graduates were being hired by the city. The most spectacular thing, however, was that there were actually Mexican Americans working for the city. They were on the police force and in the transportation departments. In the fifties, all these jobs had been filled by Anglos. Now that was changing!

I really couldn't believe it, especially when I began to hear of Mexican youth getting grants from colleges and different organizations. Before all of this, our kind had become ditch diggers, janitors, and garbage men. President Kennedy helped change all of that in the early sixties. He made many different programs available that enabled minorities to have opportunities to succeed. He sure was a great man for helping minorities.

As time went on, I saw Mexicans become judges and lawyers. I was very proud that we were finally making an impact in our society. In addition, the Anglos of this generation seemed to be a lot kinder than the ones from my generation; they were better people. I remember loving California so much that I went to visit my cousin Alicia again. This time I was grown and had my own transportation. I was at a motel in California, and my mother called me on the phone. When I answered, she greeted me and said, "Mijo, your uncle Julio is on his way to your motel to see you!"

"Okay, thank you, Mama," I said, and I hung up. I was surprised. It wasn't every day my uncle visited me at a motel. I felt a little tired but was excited to see Uncle Julio.

About an hour later, I was walking to the motel office when I saw my uncle standing there with his cowboy boots and large cowboy hat. He was wearing blue jeans and a red-and-white-striped shirt. A Mexican hillbilly, all right! He was a slender man about six feet tall. As a man in his late sixties, he looked strong for his age. He was always working on his ranch in Mexico. Most of these ranchers were healthy due to all the hard work they did.

"Hola, Tio!" I said to Uncle Julio as I approached him. "Como estas?" He smiled, and we hugged like usual. "Come back with me to Texas," I said. "My mom wants you to come and see her. I hear she'll make us some good chicken *caldo* if you do."

"Well, you know me. I love your mom's chicken soup," he said, smiling. We jumped in my car and talked about his trip and life on the ranch all the way home. When we finally got to my mother's home, she ran out and gave Uncle Julio and me huge hugs. Uncle Julio was her brother. We gave my father a huge hug as well. We sat at the table for a steaming bowl of chicken caldo. My mother, like most Mexican mothers, made a fabulous chicken soup with lots of carrots, potatoes, celery, onion, garlic, and the works. My brother, uncle, and papa must have had at least two or three servings of soup. Oh man! By the end of our dinner, we were stuffed.

"Oh, my little sister!" cried Uncle Julio. "You have always been such a tremendously good cook." My mother blushed and conversed with my uncle. They talked about our family in Mexico. It was a wonderful get-together. My brother started asking questions about my uncle's life, which prompted my uncle to invite us over to the ranch he worked on in Mexico. "You would like it," he said cheerfully. "My house is so welcoming too. You guys would be able to stay there."

No way! They couldn't pay me to go to Mexico again! I thought to myself. "Are things changing down in Mexico, Tio?" I asked my uncle.

"Of course not!" snapped my mother. "It's still the same—you know that. That's why we are here in this country." Uncle Julio's face turned a little red. He seemed embarrassed and admitted that my mother was right.

In Mexico, there are more races than just the Mexicans. Europeans, Indians, Chinese, and just about anyone you can imagine now live in Mexico. There are also a lot of Jews who own a lot of land and businesses. As for us mestizos, our fathers are the white Spaniards, and our mothers are the native Indians who once roamed the land of Mexico and the United States. Today, it seems like the Europeans still control Mexico; I mean, just look at the politicians. The rich are white and beautiful with blue eyes. They have dirty-blond hair, and all their children are delicate white flowers who are spoiled rotten. Because their parents are so rich, they don't even want to step on dirt with their pretty feet.

Europeans live the good life in Mexico. They send their children to the best schools in the United States and to other countries in the world. Beautiful blond kids with white skin roam the halls of these prestigious schools. The same things go for the rich Catholic schools near the US-Mexican border. Mexican mothers with their fair skin and beautiful jewelry drop off their children in a school where mestizos work as janitors. The Mexican Indian will starve in Mexico today. Still, the country offers no help for the poor mestizos. There's no help from the rich Mexican society. They discriminate against brown skin.

Uncle Julio talked throughout the evening. He asked me about the United States and our systems of government. I told him about the US Army and about how proud I was to be an American. Uncle Julio had great respect for this country. He told me he wished Mexico could run their country like the United States ran theirs. Perhaps the poor peasants would have to overthrow the government, as has been seen in other countries. We talked so much that we all got sleepy after a while.

When the dinner plates were cleared from the table, my mother got up and said, "Okay, time for bed—enough talking. It's very late now. Julio, you can sleep in the last room to the right. Romulo and Louis, you can share a room tonight. Goodnight." We all said buenas noches to each other and headed off to bed.

The next day, my brother and I had to go to downtown to take Uncle Julio to buy some supplies he had to take back to Mexico. We got in my '56 Ford Victoria and headed off. The car was green and white with pipes that were standard back in the day. The pipes made an underwater type of sound.

As we started to leave, my mother yelled out, "Don't forget the masa for the tortillas!" My mother would make wonderful tortillas from scratch. I think pretty much all Mexican mothers did. Before the seventies, one couldn't buy tortillas in the supermarket. As a result, people made their own tortillas, and the habit stuck for the older generations.

We went to what was called Little Mexico in downtown. They sold chili peppers, masa for tortillas, and all kinds of Mexican groceries. One could find anything from chorizo to hominy for menudo.

As we were shopping for my uncle and mother, Lloyd was walking into his and Mena's apartment drunk as a skunk. Mena was standing at the door to angrily greet him.

"What the hell is wrong with you? You were supposed to be looking for a job, not drinking!" she said with her arms firmly crossed.

Lloyd got upset. "You're always on my back! I have had it with you and your stupid family," he yelled.

"Why, Lloyd? I've tried so hard to help you. Why do you do this to me?" cried Mena.

By that time, Lloyd was in a rage. He struck Mena on the face, knocking her against the wall. Lloyd went berserk and started kicking her in the stomach and body. It seemed like the whole house was shaking. Mena was crying and yelling for help. Lloyd was yelling and cursing various types of obscenities back at her. "Shut up, you bitch!" he said fiercely. "I hate you!" It was an awful night for Mena. Lloyd had never ever done anything like that to her. He kept hitting her repeatedly. Mena was screaming and crying as she profusely bled from her face. The neighbors could hear everything.

When people came out of their apartment to see what all the fuss was about, they saw Lloyd standing over Mena, who was lying by the door in a puddle of blood. "La policia! Somebody call the cops!" Mena heard a voice scream. Instantly, Lloyd took off running. He left my poor beaten sister there like a ragdoll.

As more people poured out of their apartments and into the halls, a big strong woman by the name of Plancha ran to my sister. Now, Plancha, which translates to "Iron" in English, was a character. She was a big heavyset woman who used to work as a Mexican wrestler back in the day. She loved Mena very much because they were very close neighbors. When she saw her friend on the floor like that, she picked her up and hugged her tightly as tears poured from her heavy eyes. "What happened, Chiquita?" she cried. Her big burly arms were wrapped tightly around Mena. Mena was weak and crying like a baby. "Who did this to you?" demanded Plancha, "Was it Lloyd?"

Mena began to sob uncontrollably. After many more minutes of sobbing, she finally nodded her head.

"That son of a bitch!" screamed Plancha. "If I see him, I will tear his head off! I told you, Mena. He was no good for you. You never listened. You thought that because he's an Anglo, he was going to treat you better. Look at what happened. That lazy bum!" cried Plancha as she studied the gash on my sister's mouth.

A little while later, the police came, and Plancha offered to take my sister to the hospital. "Don't take me there, Plancha, please!" said my sister wearily. "My cuts will heal up on their own."

"If you don't go," said Plancha sternly, "I am going to have to drag you myself. Wait until your brothers find out."

"Oh no! Please don't tell them!" pleaded my sister.

"Oh, don't worry. They'll find out, and when they do, I pity whoever gets in their way! That idiot picked on the wrong woman. Plus, if I find him, it won't be pleasant for him," said Plancha.

The next day, I found what had happened to Mena when one of her neighbors came over to tell me about the incident. I was furious and wanted to destroy Lloyd. How dare he beat up my sister! My brother said, "*Vamos*, brother! Let's look for Lloyd and teach him a lesson!"

When my mother found out what had happened, she began to cry. My dad was also furious. "My little girl, Mena!" Mom screamed. She pleaded for my brother and me to not seek any type of revenge toward Lloyd. The police would eventually find him. She told us to let them take care of him because we would only make matters worse. She believed in karma and used to always say, "We reap what we sow." I felt like my head wanted to pop, I was so angry. I always saw through Lloyd and never trusted him. Nevertheless, I hung on to what mother had said.

Days passed, and we looked for Lloyd all over the neighborhood. Even the cops could not find him, though they weren't trying very hard. It seemed like the dirt had swallowed him whole. My sister was slowly recovering. She had one broken rib, which I suppose was from Lloyd's kick, and many cuts and bruises on her face. *Wait till I get hold of him to see how he fights with a man*, I often told myself. More days passed, and nothing happened. I figured he must have gone back to the mountains in Tennessee.

After about a month, Uncle Javier invited my brother, my sister, and me to have some menudo at his house. He was the neighborhood barber, and everybody liked him; he was a kind of town celebrity. He was a tall and heavyset man who always wore a suit and a tie. His pants were always ironed, and his shoes were neatly polished.

His hair was gently combed back, and he sported a well-trimmed mustache. He looked very sophisticated with his rimmed glasses. When we would walk through the neighborhood with my uncle as kids, everybody would greet him. Uncle Javier was well educated, and he spoke Spanish very well. He had studied in Mexico and liked his barber profession. One could talk to him about any subject, and Uncle Javier seemed to know it all. When I talked to him in Spanish, he would often correct the way I pronounced things. "No, mijo. You must pronounce this word like this." He helped me nail the right pronunciations and learn the correct Spanish grammar.

Uncle Javier's house was nice and clean, a little light brown house right in the center of the neighborhood. His wife was a schoolteacher born in the United States and of Mexican descent. She was a nice, educated lady who had a daughter in college. Everybody was so proud of that daughter. Remember that Latinos going to college was still a fairly new thing back in those days.

We all sat down at the table in the small but neatly cleaned kitchen. The table was dressed with a yellow cloth. We ate from big brown bowls filled with steaming menudo and wonderful, good-smelling spices. We also had small french rolls to dip in our menudo. We ate very well that night; it was so good and delicious. We ate and talked about all subjects. Javier's wife Adela was very educated and talked about very interesting things. She also talked about the recipe for young Latinos to get ahead: education. "Thank God that my daughter is going to have that chance."

Uncle Javier always had money, and if he saw someone in a bad situation, he would always offer some type of help. He was a generous man, but he also knew how to manage his money. He would often say, "It's not about how much money you make—it's how you manage the money that counts. I have seen men make good money, and in a few days they are broke. I have seen others with small paychecks who seem to always have money. Sometimes I even see them lend money to those who make good money. Be wise with your money! Learn to budget." Needless to say, I learned a lot from him. He was a wise man.

After eating, we thanked Uncle Javier and Adela for a wonderful meal. We hugged, my brother left to my mother's house, and I headed for my apartment. I was stuffed and slept like a baby.

It was early in the morning when I heard a hard knock on my door. I was still half asleep. Confused, I wondered who on earth it could be. I opened the door and saw my sister, Mena, standing there and crying hysterically. "What happened, hermana?" I asked. "Tell me!"

She was crying so hard that she couldn't speak. I took her by the hand and hugged her. I led her into my apartment and sat her down on a small sofa. I then tried to calm her down so she could tell me what happened. She was awfully pale. "Are you sick or something, sister? Talk to me! What happened?" I said.

Still crying, she started to say, "Brother, Lloyd is dead!"

"What?" I said, shocked. "What happened?"

She started crying harder. "The police came over to the house and asked me to go identify his body. I went, and it was him," said my sister. Lloyd had apparently gone to Mexico and stayed with this woman he had met there. The woman had been married, and the husband had been away for work purposes. That particular day, the husband had come back home and found Lloyd and his wife in bed together, and he'd shot them both dead. The police had arrested the husband and transferred Lloyd's body back to the States.

I thought to myself, *What a shocker!* They transferred the body with no problems. It was nothing like what we'd gone through with Uncle Carlos's body. My sister loved Lloyd so much. I would have given Lloyd a good ass kicking, but other than that, I wouldn't have done anything else to him. I felt bad for my sister for loving this man. Life was going to be hard for her.

Mena would stay with my mother and father so that they could comfort and look after her. I was stunned. I guess the police would contact his family somehow. Days and weeks passed, and these unfortunate events were the talk of the neighborhood. There was nothing the police could do; Mexico was another country. I had heard and seen very violent acts in that country. Even today, I'm so glad that my folks left that place. I was lucky that nothing ever happened to me while I was over there.

My sister suffered a lot after what happened to Lloyd. It took her a lot of time and tears to be able to overcome this tragedy. After a year and half, she felt all the weight off her shoulders. Like they say, as time passes, the wounds begin to heal.

I remember walking inside a grocery store one day and seeing tortillas. This made me laugh because the only tortillas that anyone ever saw were the homemade ones that the neighborhood Mexican moms made. Now I knew that it couldn't only be Mexicans who liked tortillas. One wouldn't think that Anglo people liked Mexican food back in those days. Well, surprise! Not only were Anglos found to like spicy Mexican food, but they were even learning how to make Mexican dishes. Oh boy! As they say, life is full of surprises!

One of the coolest guys I had ever known was named Jessie. He was an Anglo and a real kind-hearted guy. We became good buddies. There was a time when Jessie and I were having an argument about who had labeled the Mexican Americans in the United States Chicanos. I said that I'd heard it was none other than President Lyndon Johnson. This president lived in a county in East Texas. There were a lot of Mexicans who lived there, and he didn't even know how to speak or understand Spanish. What a laugh! Of course, in those little towns, they still looked at us Mexicans like dogs.

There were signs hanging on walls of stores and restaurants in East Texas that read, "No dogs or Mexicans allowed." Racism seemed to be more prominent in East Texas than in West Texas.

Jessie began to ask me more about President Johnson. I told him about a story I had heard a few years back. They said that when President Johnson was in his home town, he had one of those white convertible Cadillacs. One day he was driving it fast through the muddy roads of the countryside. He was singing and yelling out the country songs blaring loudly on the radio with a six pack of beer at his side.

At that time, there was a rookie cop who spotted him driving recklessly. He pulled the president over to the side of the road. The cop got off his motorcycle with his dark sunglasses on. Striding pompously to the president's car, he flexed his chest like all the cops do. He did not recognize the president at first and asked for his driver's license. The president didn't budge. Finally, the cop asked him again for his license in a commanding voice. When the cop got closer, he froze and said, "Oh my God!"

The president smirked and answered, "That's right, son. It's me, and don't you forget it." Needless to say, the cop apologized for interrupting the president's joyride and let him go. Jessie couldn't stop laughing when I told him that story. Who knows if that is really a true story? But we all believed it when we were told it.

One sunny afternoon, Jessie and I went to a grocery store that was supposed to be classy and well organized. It was an all-Anglo store from what we could tell because we didn't see any Mexicans. As we walked into the store, right in the corner was a little stand, like a popcorn machine stand. However, it was not a popcorn machine stand—it was a nacho stand! They were selling nachos! I couldn't believe it! They only used to sell those in the Mexican stores. Was I seeing things? *Nobody here is going to buy those,* I thought. It seemed like nobody was interested. I don't think Anglos knew what nachos were. Jessie and I laughed and proceeded to buy what we needed to buy at the store. Afterward, we headed toward the line at the cashier. There was nothing but Anglo people ahead of me, and leading the line was a Mexican man and his wife. This man had a little white tray full of nachos oozing cheese.

By golly, he was eating them so sloppily and making lots of crunchy noises. To top it off, this Mexican guy opened his mouth real wide and pitched in several nachos all at once. All the Anglo people in those times were very finicky. They were staring at him in disgust as if he was insulting the world by eating nachos like that! This Mexican guy made Jessie and me laugh.

This Mexican guy was probably the only person in the store who bought those nachos, and I'm sure those Anglos were fascinated by what he was eating; it was strange to them. Additionally, this Mexican was the typical guy from Mexico. He had a head full of bushy black hair and a large bushy mustache to match. He even had a gold tooth that flashed every time he opened his big mouth. Heck, I found myself staring too!

When it was his turn to pay, the Mexican guy grabbed another big nacho, dripping with cheese. He tried to put it into his wife's mouth, but she refused. I could tell she was embarrassed by his actions, especially when she was getting her purse to pay the cashier. Still, he was trying to put that nacho into her mouth even with the cashier looking at them in disgust. The lady tightened her lips to refuse the nacho the man kept trying to shove into her mouth. Still, he didn't seem to get the message. To top it off, this line was long, and the lady couldn't seem to find her change.

The Anglos were beginning to get impatient and angry. Jessie and I couldn't do anything but laugh at the comedy scene taking place in front of us. It's funny thinking about this. Now there are nacho stands all over the place! Before Jessie and I left the store, we had to get us some nachos too! We gave the nacho lady some business besides the one Mexican man. I sure hoped she made a successful business. As it turned out, it took a few more years for Anglos to accept nachos. I am sure if they put a Mexican restaurant in Europe, they would get rich. It's hard to believe Mexican food is all over the United States now. Times have changed so much, especially in the way that people think. Back when I was young, the Anglos were very prejudiced. Maybe it was because many Mexicans coming into the United States were poor, uneducated people.

I am so glad this wonderful country gave my parents the opportunity to become American citizens. There is no telling how much abuse my parents would have encountered in Mexico. Some people in Mexico might feel offended by my sentiments. I sometimes get asked, "Aren't you a Mexican?" I always respond with, "No, I am not Mexican—I am a Mexican American." You see, I love the Mexican people, but it is the country and its system that I despise. There are good and bad people everywhere, of course. That country was only made for the rich to prosper and the poor to falter.

It is truly survival of the fittest there, even if it means stepping on each other's neck to get ahead. Unfortunately, things have not changed there. It is really sad. There was another day when my mother invited Jessie and me to eat enchiladas, Jessie's favorite plate. My mother loved to cook, and she was always inviting people to the house to eat. She loved people and was a kind lady who loved God. Friends and relatives of my mother would always come over for her advice and comfort. After Jessie and I ate, we decided to take a stroll through downtown in my old '56 Ford Victoria. The whole time, we listened to rock and roll music and reminisced about the good old days. It was a Saturday evening, and all the people were in town. This was the place to come on weekends because downtown had so many theaters and bars. Stores in downtown were open much later than they are now, and this kept a lot of people roaming for hours. So many things have changed. Texas used to have a lot of industry, such as factories that produced blue jeans, fabrics, boxes, and many other different items. After all, Texas has more cotton fields than any other US state and produces approximately 25 percent of the country's cotton crop. Many girls who worked in these factories would come downtown on Saturdays.

There was a park in the center of town that we called Animal Park. In the center of the park was a small, circular, bricklike fence. On the other side of the fence, there were live alligators for public entertainment. There were always two or three alligators, and bunches of people would gather around to watch them. Lots of simple, pretty girls would make eye contact with the guys. Because of this, it was my and Jessie's favorite hangout. I wonder why? In the park, we would see people joyfully eating ice cream and popcorn. Small kids would be running, yelling, and laughing with joy. It was fun. It seemed like the people in that era had more happiness. They didn't have the face of stress that people have nowadays and seemed much happier than now. I'll bet it's because money in those days went further than it goes now. With twenty dollars, you could get so many groceries that you could fill up your refrigerator. With two dollars, you could practically fill up your gas tank.

Jessie and I had been eyeballing a couple of chicks when I heard somebody call out, "Louie!" It was none other than Slugger, who had been a good friend of mine for some time. "What's going on, Slugger?" I said, happy to see him. Slugger had a boxing gym in town. He was a guy about five foot eight and 155 pounds.

He had been a boxer and had been named amateur champion in the welterweight division in Mexico. He loved to wear white polo shirts with khaki pants. One could often see his big forearms with those short-sleeved shirts he liked to wear. They were very impressive because they were muscular, and the veins seemed to pop out like blue snakes. He was a tough old boy. I thought that if people ever dared to mess with this guy, they'd better watch out! However, as long as one didn't mess with him, he was a hell of a nice guy. He was a good-looking guy for being a fighter—no scars on his face.

"When are you guys going to come by my gym? You know you are welcome anytime. Right now, I'm training a couple of professional fighters. I still train in the Golden Gloves," said Slugger. Slugger was a few years older than Jessie and me. He always had a smile on his face unless somebody made him angry.

"Hey, what happened last time? You said you caught a taxi from Mexico to Texas." I said, changing the subject.

"Yeah, I did, because I didn't feel like walking that bridge," laughed Slugger. "I was a little tired." Slugger told us about how he'd asked this taxi driver how much would it cost to get him across the bridge from Mexico to Texas in his taxi. The taxi driver told him it was five dollars. When they got to the States, Slugger got out of the taxi and handed the cab driver five dollars. The driver then began to yell, "I told you it was ten dollars! Not five!" Slugger reminded him that he had told him five dollars initially, and the taxi driver told Slugger he changed his mind. "Now it's ten dollars."

"That's not my fault," Slugger told the driver.

The driver got furious. "You're going to pay me, or I'll knock you on your ass!" he screamed angrily as he got out of the car. The driver was a big guy, at least 250 pounds. He didn't know Slugger had been a professional fighter.

"Okay, let's go, *vato*!" said Slugger.

The taxi driver, thinking he was so big and powerful, took a swing at Slugger. What a great mistake! Slugger ducked and gave the driver a beautiful uppercut to his broad chin. The guy went down like a ton of bricks. He was knocked out completely!

Needless to say, all the border patrol guys and cops came rushing down. They were hollering and yelling, like they usually do. "What is going on?" screamed one cop. It was a big mess, and the cops wanted to put Slugger in jail. Slugger said one of the cops knew him and asked what had happened. Slugger had trained this cop in boxing, so he believed Slugger. "If it wasn't for this cop I personally knew, they would have arrested me," Slugger said.

Later on, that cop came up to Slugger and said, "I saw that uppercut you gave that taxi driver. You've got to teach me that one!"

That was Slugger for you. He didn't like to fight on the streets, only in the ring. A lot of times, there are folks who don't know who they're provoking. You learn many of these things the tough way. I told Slugger that I would visit his gym one of these days to train. We parted, and Jessie and I headed out to a bar to have a beer. We made our way into a nice, classy bar that seemed like the kind to serve cocktails. The people in there seemed civilized. Good thing I never drank much; I always had bad memories of what had happened to my uncle Carlos. Intoxication is dangerous, and I didn't believe in losing control because anything could happen. Jessie and I sat on a small cushy sofa by some tables. The lounge had red walls with mirrors. There was a good-looking, classic jukebox standing across from us. The lounge was jumping with joy, as they say.

On the tall bar stools were guys and girls sitting and laughing. All through the night, they enjoyed themselves and the music, which wasn't too loud; one could talk and enjoy the conversation. Oldies but goodies were playing from the jukebox. The atmosphere was much calmer than that of one of those cheap bars. This was probably the best club in Texas. Because the other bars were really crowded, we really couldn't enjoy ourselves in them like we could in here.

The owner of this bar always had civilized clients. You didn't have to worry about somebody making a trophy of your head with a beer bottle. The other half of the club was a small restaurant. You could walk in with your lady to the back of the club for a snack or a good meal. Those days were more enjoyable for all of us. Everybody had a job, and although the jobs didn't pay much, you could still afford a reasonable living.

As time passed, my parents passed on to heaven. It was sad to say goodbye to each of them, but nothing is forever. I will always remember their good upbringing. My sister, my brother, and I will always be grateful for their great love toward us. My brother, Romulo, went to work for the city as a police officer, and my sister remarried a kind gentleman who was hardworking and responsible.

As for me, I got hired to work for the city as well, though in a department different from the one my brother worked in. I couldn't believe that I was a mestizo working for the city. I was so proud! Needless to say, my brother and I retired from the city after many years of employment. Now, in these modern years, you can see the courthouse full of Mexican Americans as judges, lawyers, and commissioners and in other good-standing jobs all over the cities of Texas and across the country.

The days of mestizos destined to be only janitors and low-paid workers are disappearing. Our time has finally come, especially for our new generation of Mexican Americans. Many continue to seek higher education in preparation for successful careers as they learn to let go of self-inferiority and look forward to being Americans with all the hopes and dreams that this country stands for. The only sad thing is that Mexico will probably continue to be what it is and was: a corrupt, mean country that exploits its' people. People to this day are still trying to get out of there. Now it seems worse with the drug cartels, gangs, drugs, murders, and corrupted government. My heart aches for these people. We should be so blessed to be here in the United States, where there are laws and protection.

The small town I grew up in is now like a ghost town. People have moved up and on for better opportunities elsewhere. To see it now brings me great sorrow. Still, small-town Texas had its good ol' days. People from south of the border and the military enjoyed themselves here at one point. The great entertainment of theaters, which at one time were so ubiquitous that they were just a block or two apart from each other, is now gone. My small town in Texas has quite a bit of history. Many of the young educated people had to leave this town to make it in the world.

All the industries that used to be here moved to Mexico for its cheap labor. American factories, which provided the people of this Texas town with many jobs, vanished. Like I said, times have changed. I am still here, though, reminiscing about my fond memories of my youth. I'm an old man grateful for what I have and for the wonderful life God has granted me. If by chance you happen to be strolling by, come and visit! I will tell you many more exciting stories of the small town in Texas in which I grew up. However, I must urge you not to get too disappointed by what you see. Just remember that at one time, this small Texas town was flourishing with life, full of businesses, jobs, family, and love.

Printed in the United States
by Booksellers

Printed in the United States
By Bookmasters